FLOWERS
FOR BORDERS

CHANCELLOR
PRESS

Acknowledgements

This book has been compiled with material previously published by Reed International Books.

Text by Suzy Powling. Additional text by Meg Sanders. Illustrations by Vicky Emptage and Patrick Tate. Symbols by Coryn Dickman.

The publishers would like to thank the following organizations and individuals for their kind permission to reproduce the photographs in this book:

Pat Brindley 46, 61; Eric Crichton 20; Garden Picture Library/Derek Fell 26; Tania Midgley 70; Natural History Photographic Agency/M Savonius 40; Reed International Books Ltd/Michael Boys 23, 30, 58/Jerry Harpur, 12, 21, 24, 31, 32, 35, 36, 41, 42, 43, 44, 45, 47, 48, 49, 50, 52, 55, 57, 59, 60, 65, 69, 71/Neil Holmes 62, 67/George Wright 22, 25, 28, 29, 34, 37, 38, 39, 51, 53, 54, 56, 64, 66, 68; Harry Smith Collection 27, 33, 63

First published in Great Britain in 1995
by Chancellor Press, an imprint of Reed Consumer Books Limited
Michelin House, 81 Fulham Road, London SW3 6RB
and Auckland, Melbourne, Singapore and Toronto

ISBN 1 85152 626 9

A catalogue record for this book is available from the British Library.

Produced by Mandarin Offset, Hong Kong
Printed in Hong Kong

CONTENTS

PREPARATION & PLANNING

Gardening is one of life's most creative activities. Whether a garden extends to several acres or is confined to a few square yards, the gardener brings it to life, deciding what to plant and where, what to move – and sometimes what to discard.

All these decisions are affected by certain factors that must be taken into account in order to achieve success. The most important of these are climate, site and soil. To a large extent you must work with what you are given – human beings have no control over the weather, for example – and it is essential to identify these factors before you can accommodate or improve them.

CLIMATE Climate includes many variables – rainfall, humidity, temperature, wind and intensity of light – which influence the kind of plants that will thrive in the region where you live. The first factor to take into account is whether a particular plant can withstand the lowest temperatures likely to occur. Most of the plants described in this book are hardy in temperate zones, meaning that they need no protection at any point in their life cycle - provided you live in a temperate zone. Some, however, will only thrive against a warm, sunny wall. Half-hardy plants need protection during the winter, such as a cloche or a covering of straw or hessian; tender plants need permanent protection such as that afforded by a green-house, but a few can be set outside in the heat of summer.

There are plants with particular likes and dislikes, such as clematis, which likes a cool root run, or camellia, which should not be placed where early morning sun after frost might damage young growth. To help a plant give of its best, it is important to observe these individual requirements. Plant some *Alchemilla mollis* where it will cast shade over the roots of a clematis, and do not site your camellia on a wall that gets the morning sun.

RAINFALL Excessive rainfall causes a problem in gardens where drainage is poor, though this can sometimes be corrected. Even so it may make life difficult for plants like alpines and others that like a sunny, dry bank. Some flowers are badly damaged by rain – white roses, for example – and wind after rain can be devastating. Lack of rain is a more general problem. In areas where rainfall is low, it makes sense to concentrate on plants that can cope with drought and to use moisture-retentive mulches of peat, leaf-mould, spent hops, garden compost, well-rotted manure or pulverized bark on plants that need it – particularly shrubs, roses, dahlias and sweet peas.

SUN AND SHADE There are many splendid plants that will only give of their best if they receive a full day's sunshine. However, many more will be sustained by just a few hours every day, and most gardens, however ill-favoured they seem, will enjoy some sunshine for at least part of the day. The blessing is that there are so many desirable plants that prefer shade or semi-shade. Take note of the source of the shade and plan accordingly: a large tree will not only cast a correspondingly large shadow, but take all the nutrients from the soil around it, so that no other plants can thrive. A shaded wall will be cool but need not be bare: clematis, jasmine, honeysuckles and some roses will do well in such a situation.

WINDS Occasional fierce winds are a hazard most gardeners try to become philosophical about. On sites where strong winds are a more regular feature, it makes sense to erect barriers in the form of quick-growing dense hedges or fences that can be clothed with climbers - both are better than brick walls, which can trap pockets of frost. Flowering shrubs suitable for hedging include deutzia, forsythia, fuchsia, lavender, pyracantha, roses, santolina, lilac and viburnum.

SOILS There is no such thing as a perfect soil. Just like the weather, there is always something for gardeners to complain about. But at least improving your soil is a possibility. Different plants can have very different soil requirements, so before you start planting, it is vital to have some understanding of your soil type. A little investigation will help ensure that you are working with, rather than against, nature and making the best of the conditions in your garden.

There are four basic soil types – sand, loam, clay or peat – and they may be heavy, medium or light, well drained or waterlogged, well cultivated or neglected. These are things you can usually tell just by observation and feel. A sandy soil, for example, will feel gritty to the touch and is generally light to dig and free draining. Clay looks shiny if rubbed and has a dense texture. It will stick to your boots in wet conditions and will feel heavy to dig. Loam falls somewhere in between these two extremes and, as such, is the closest thing to an ideal all-round soil that it is possible to find. Peat is an organic soil, dark with a spongy, fibrous texture. It is often acid and may be slow to drain. Another variant is chalky soil, which is easily identified by the whitish subsoil, sometimes with chunks of chalk visible. Despite the variety of types, you can improve most soils simply by adding plenty of well-rotted organic matter, and incorporating grit if the soil is heavy and poor draining.

In addition to their basic types, soils can be acid or alkaline and this is something you can test for using a simple kit, available from garden centres. Soil pH, as it is called, is hard to change and will certainly affect your choice of plants. A chalky or limy soil is said to be alkaline and it will give a reading of above pH7, usually shown by a blue coloration in the test sample. Neutral is pH7, indicated by a green colour, while acid readings of below pH6.5 will be shown by a red or orange shade.

Plants like rhododendrons and heathers thrive on acid soils and do very badly on limy sites. Pinks and clematis relish limy, alkaline conditions. Most plants grow well on a neutral soil. You can help neutralize an acid soil by adding lime, but it is very difficult to bring down the pH of an alkaline soil, although adding organic matter can help.

Garden compost or well rotted farmyard manure is an excellent source of organic matter, but leaf mould and grass clippings can also be used. Even a small garden can yield a reasonable amount of compost. The secret is to vary the ingredients so that air circulation is possible, with coarse as well as soft material – for example, straw as well as grass clippings in 20cm/8in layers. In three to six months, you should have a crumbly, dark brown mixture that will do wonders for any soil.

DESIGN AND SHAPES OF BORDERS Whether you are developing an entirely new garden or altering an established one, you are unlikely to have a completely free choice about the siting of beds and borders. There will certainly be functional areas to consider – a drying area, a children's play area, a sitting area, parking, paths and access, perhaps a vegetable patch or fruit cage – and any or all of these may take priority over your flower borders.

Once these elements have been fitted in, the flower gardener makes what is possible of the remaining space, but even so there are considerations of site, sun, shade and shelter that may influence your decision. Before you start digging, spend a while observing the conditions in your garden – after a while the siting of borders will seem an obvious, perhaps almost inevitable, choice.

The type of borders you establish will depend on the style of garden you want to create – this, also, may be dictated by the style of your house or the shape of the plot. The two basic categories are formal and informal, but within these there is ample scope for variety and self-expression. Formal layouts are generally based on symmetrical and regular geometric shapes – a square or rectangular lawn with rectangular beds surrounding it, for example. Circles and ellipses are possible, too, but must be clearly defined and regular. Informal plans are popular in small gardens as they can give an impression of space, and the pinnacle of informal garden design is seen in tiny cottage gardens where plants of all types are crammed together in soft drifts of colour and form, and all edges are blurred. In informal gardens, the margins between lawn, paths and beds are always ambiguous and curves are soft and flowing.

Achieving these different looks involves specific techniques at the construction stage. For example, geometric shapes must be laid out strictly with careful measurements, making sure each element is centred visually. Circles are best described by fixing a cane at the centre point and tying on a piece of twine the length of the radius. This, in turn, is tied to the neck of a bottle of silver sand and, by keeping the string taut and walking round the cane, trickling sand as you go, you will produce a perfect circle. In informal gardens, measurements are less important. Try marking out the shapes of beds and borders by laying a hosepipe on the ground. It can be moved and adjusted to give just the curve you want and, if you leave it in place on the lawn for a few days, the grass underneath will yellow slightly, giving you a clear line to cut along to form the border.

Although many gardens have traditionally been based on the idea of long borders around the edges, backed by walls or hedges, island beds have gained in popularity and give an opportunity for exciting design and planting. Obviously, borders are viewed from the front and the traditional and perfectly logical way of designing them is to place the tallest plants at the back and the smallest at the front. Island beds, however, can be viewed from all sides and have to be planted with this in mind. The taller plants will, of course, be placed in the middle with the smaller ones at the edges. This has the very desirable effect of concealing parts of the garden from view and creating a slight air of mystery that can otherwise be hard to achieve in a small plot.

In large, estate gardens, where battalions of gardeners were employed to labour away all year round, enormous herbaceous borders were commonly established, providing a glorious display in summer and a great deal of work for the rest of the year. When gardening on a small scale, continuity of display is as important as keeping maintenance to a manageable level. More practical than herbaceous borders are mixed borders, where shrubs, herbaceous plants, biennials, annuals and bulbs all play a part. In a true cottage garden, fruit and vegetables would also be included, squeezed in wherever there was a space.

Mixed borders lend themselves equally well to formal and informal plantings, but the choice of plants will, of course, differ. Another advantage of this type of planting is that it can be adapted to different aspects – there are few annuals, for example, that really do well in shade, so a shaded bed can be based around carefully selected, shade-tolerant shrubs and perennials, with bulbs for low-level interest and pockets of annuals, such as meconopsis, which thrive in semi-shaded conditions. In sunny beds, annuals and perennials can provide flowering interest in summer, with variegated evergreen and winter-flowering shrubs and bulbs taking over for the rest of the year.

PLANTING

Once you have assessed your soil and situation, negotiated areas of the garden for your flower borders and drawn up a plan, you can get down to the enjoyable business of buying and planting your selected specimens. Pot-grown plants are on sale in many retail outlets these days, and it is impossible to generalize about quality, but there are some signs to watch out for when buying plants. Avoid any with obvious pests or diseases, broken or damaged shoots, dried-up and shrunken soil, or profuse weed growth around the base of the plant. Remove the plant from its pot and look at the roots. If the base of the soil ball is completely taken up with twisted roots the plant is pot-bound and will be unlikely to thrive when planted. Roots that fill the soil ball are a good sign, provided they are light in colour, plump and firm. If the soil ball falls apart, the plant has only recently been potted on from a smaller container and is not ready to be planted out.

Plants are available in other forms, too; bare-rooted for roses and some shrubs in early spring, or in polythene bags with moist peat or sawdust for perennials and some bulbs. These are quite satisfactory, provided the plants have been well cared for and have not been in storage for too long.

Planting in early to mid-spring is safe for hardy perennials, while evergreen shrubs, which are usually pot-grown, can be planted in mid-autumn or mid-spring. Do not plant out half-hardy plants until late spring, when you can be reasonably sure that there will be no more frosts. Deciduous shrubs can be planted during the dormant season, provided conditions are suitable.

Before planting, all perennial weeds should have been removed and the ground well dug over. Dig a planting hole about twice as wide as the root ball or root spread of the plant, and about 1cm/½in deeper. Fork over the bottom of the hole and add a handful of bone meal to the soil you have removed. Water your plant thoroughly, then remove it from the container or packaging. Place it in the hole, adjusting the depth if necessary, then fill in the soil around it, firming with gentle pressure from your heel, and water in well *(see overleaf)*.

In spring, most shrubs and perennial plants benefit greatly from a top dressing of balanced fertilizer, such as fish, blood and bone, favoured by organic gardeners, or a faster-acting formulation such as John Innes or Growmore. These supply a fairly equal amount of the three main plant nutrients,

13

Planting a containerized border plant

N (nitrogen), P (phosphate) and K (potassium), and will help your plants put on healthy growth each year. Remember, also, to water new plants regularly, in particular during dry spells in the growing season.

PEST AND DISEASE CONTROL The best way of coping with pests and diseases is to discourage outbreaks by providing optimal growing conditions for your plants and inspecting them regularly, so that prompt action can be taken. In the right situation and with appropriate feeding and watering, most plants will be growing vigorously enough to withstand mild attacks and to recover quickly once you have dealt with the source of trouble.

Not all pests are worth bothering with. For example, leaf hoppers on roses are difficult to eradicate and cause only minor pale mottling of the foliage. Aphids, on the other hand, can transmit viruses to your previously healthy plants and it can take nerves of steel to wait for the ladybirds to turn up and save the day. Slugs and snails can cause considerable damage to newly emerging soft shoots, but can be dealt with in a variety of ways. Refer to pages 72-3 to help you diagnose what the problem is before taking any action.

Pests can be killed chemically, but at the risk of damaging beneficial insects and upsetting your garden ecology; they can be controlled naturally by encouraging their predators, ranging from hedgehogs and toads for slugs down to hoverflies and ladybirds for aphids; or in some cases they can be discouraged by physical barriers, such as sharp sand sprinkled around slug-susceptible plants.

Diseases are more difficult to eradicate without resorting to chemicals. Growing the plants well is the first, fundamental step; never knowingly introducing diseased stock is the next, but who would? You can reduce the risk by not accepting cuttings from neighbours but, even so, diseases will occur. Once again, regular checks will allow you to take speedy action. Some types of infection can be cut out, but often spraying is the only answer. In some cases, once disease sets in, entire plants may have to be destroyed. When using any garden chemicals, follow the manufacturers' instructions to the letter and only spray on a dry, still day when you will have the best chance of controlling the way in which you apply the chemical.

PROPAGATION

Raising your own plants is a tremendously satisfying process, and can provide new material for very little expense. Different methods are suitable for different types of plants.

CUTTINGS Cuttings may be taken from various parts of a plant. Hardwood cuttings are used for shrubs and are taken between autumn and spring. Semi-ripe cuttings are used for increasing shrubs, and soft cuttings are used to propagate many perennials and sub-shrubs, like pelargoniums.

The size of the cuttings and the best time of year to take them are given in the individual plant entries.

SOFT CUTTINGS These are immature non-flowering shoot tips. Make a sharp cut just below a node and remove the bottom pair of leaves before placing the cutting in the rooting medium. Soft cuttings take 10-30 days to take root.

SEMI-RIPE CUTTINGS These are firmer than soft cuttings. They are usually taken in summer and do not need added heat; a cold frame is the best environment. Take a cutting from a healthy side shoot, if necessary with a heel, a small piece of older wood attached. Cleanly cut off the soft tip and remove the lowest pair of leaves before inserting in the rooting medium. The cuttings should be ready for planting out in nursery rows the following spring.

HARDWOOD CUTTINGS Take a cutting between 15 and 37cm/6 and 15in long. Remove all but the top three pairs of leaves. If there is an unripened shoot at the tip, cut back to a suitable bud. Take out a V-shaped trench 25cm/10in deep in good, weed-free soil and place a shallow layer of sand at the bottom to assist drainage. Insert the cuttings to half to two-thirds their length and push the soil back. Plant very firmly. Leave for at least a year before transferring to the permanent positions.

DIVISION Most perennials are increased by division. Lift the plant when dormant – between autumn and spring. Separate the sections by hand, trowel or two forks *(below)* in

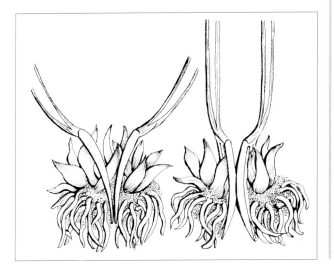

the case of larger plants. Discard the central, woody sections and replant the outer parts.

RAISING PLANTS FROM SEED Most plants can be raised from seed, though some take literally years to germinate. You will find it useful to raise most of your annuals in this way. Seeds of hardy annuals may be sown outside in spring in a well-prepared bed. Water the soil the day before. Mark out shallow drills with the side of a hoe, sow the seed thinly along the row and cover lightly with soil. Water well with a fine rose the day after sowing and again a week later.

Half-hardy annuals can be raised from seed sown indoors from spring onwards. Fill a seed tray with moist seed compost and press down evenly and firmly. Place the seeds on top, cover with 5mm/¼in of sifted compost and water in gently until the compost is thoroughly wet. Cover with a sheet of glass or polythene and place in a heated frame or propagator. As soon as the seed leaves appear, remove the cover and move to a protected position in the light.

PRICKING OUT When the true leaves appear the seedlings can be pricked off into trays or 7.5cm/3in pots of potting compost. Prepare planting holes with a pencil, spacing them 4cm/1½in apart. Carefully remove a small clump of seedlings with a plastic plant tag or similar tool, holding them by the leaves, never the roots. Separate them gently and lower them one by one into the planting holes. Use a pencil to firm the compost around each one. Water in using a fine rose watering can. Place the tray in a cold frame or on a windowsill away from direct sunlight for two to three days, then move into a sunlit position. Harden off the seedlings gradually by exposing them to increasing amounts of fresh air during the day. When they are hardened off they may be planted in their permanent positions.

LAYERING Some plants layer themselves naturally and a number of other plants, particularly shrubs, can be persuaded to reproduce themselves in this way. Autumn is the best time. Prepare the soil by digging it over. Select a healthy one-year-old non-flowering branch. Remove a portion of leaves from the stem. Make a shallow sloping cut in the underside of the branch. Bend it at the cut, without breaking the stem, and place the cut portion on the ground. Peg it in place, with the growing tip pointing upwards. Cover the cut with compost and water in. Healthy roots should have developed from the cut within a year. At this point the branch can be severed from its parent and set in its permanent position.

A-Z of FLOWERS FOR BORDERS

ANNUALS
PERENNIALS
BULBS
SHRUBS

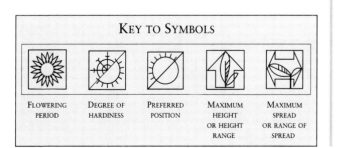

KEY TO SYMBOLS

| FLOWERING PERIOD | DEGREE OF HARDINESS | PREFERRED POSITION | MAXIMUM HEIGHT OR HEIGHT RANGE | MAXIMUM SPREAD OR RANGE OF SPREAD |

ANTIRRHINUM

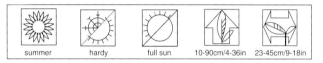

| summer | hardy | full sun | 10-90cm/4-36in | 23-45cm/9-18in |

Commonly known as snapdragon, *Antirrhinum majus* is a perennial usually treated as an annual, although in very favoured areas it may survive the winter. Modern varieties are available in all colours except blue, and the profuse tubular flowers look stunning in a summer border. They also make good cut flowers.

PROPAGATION Sow seeds in very early spring indoors with gentle heat. Prick the seedlings out into boxes when they are large enough to handle and harden off before planting out in late spring. Alternatively raise plants during the summer in a cold frame for planting out the following year.

GROWING A well-drained soil, previously enriched with well-rotted compost, is best. Pinch out growing tips to encourage bushy growth, unless single stems are required for cutting. Dead-head regularly.

VARIETIES Always choose rust-resistant varieties from the following divisions. 'Maximum', up to 90cm/3ft, many colours – the Rocket group is a vigorous strain; 'Nanum', up to 45cm/18in – 'Cheerio' is a sturdy hybrid; 'Pumilum', dwarfs at 15cm/6in. 'Tom Thumb Mixed' and 'Pixie' are reliable types which may also be grown in the rock garden.

POSSIBLE PROBLEMS Rust is the major problem. Aphids may damage young shoots.

CHRYSANTHEMUM

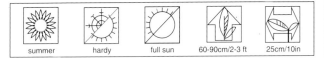

| summer | hardy | full sun | 60-90cm/2-3 ft | 25cm/10in |

Chrysanthemums comprise a huge family of very varied plants. The most popular annual variety, *Chrysanthemum carinatum*, has bright green, coarsely dissected leaves and cheerful daisy-like blooms 5cm/2in or more across. Petals yellow at the base and banded in pink and white, red or purple radiate from a flat, purple, central disc. Double-flowered versions are available. The species *C. coronarium* has a yellow centre and yellow and white flowers. *C maximum (above)* has single white flowers with yellow centres and toothed leaves. Annual chrysanthemums prolong the life of the summer border by flowering well into the autumn.

PROPAGATION Sow seed directly into the flowering site towards the end of spring, and thin the seedlings to 25cm/10in when large enough to handle. In warmer areas, an autumn sowing – protected with cloches over winter – gives large, earlier blooms the following year.

GROWING Chrysanthemums like fertile, well-drained soil and a sunny position. Pinch out the first growing tips to encourage long side stems for cutting. Although the stems are strong, supporting canes may be advisable on windy sites.

VARIETIES 'Monarch Court Jesters', many colours, single flowers; 'Flore-Plenum', yellow/white, compact double flowers

POSSIBLE PROBLEMS Aphids and earwigs can be problems.

21

CONVOLVULUS

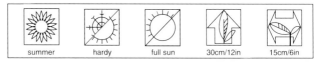

| summer | hardy | full sun | 30cm/12in | 15cm/6in |

Mediterranean in origin, *Convolvulus tricolor* is a garden relative of bindweed, though happily much less rampant. Like its other familiar cousin, ipomoea (morning glory), it bears open, trumpet-shaped blue flowers which appear throughout the summer and (unlike morning glory) stay open all day.

PROPAGATION Sow seed in the open in spring, covering with cloches to protect from cold until the plants are established. Thin seedlings to 12cm/5in when they reach 5cm/2in in height.

GROWING Give *C. tricolor* a sheltered site on ordinary, well-drained soil. Keep the young plants free of weeds. Remove faded flowerheads to ensure a succession of blooms.

VARIETIES 'Blue Flash' (*above*), dwarf variety, bushy plants, deep blue flower with yellow and white eye; 'Crimson Monarch', cherry-red flowers; 'Sky Blue', light blue.

DIANTHUS

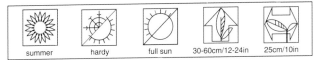

| summer | hardy | full sun | 30-60cm/12-24in | 25cm/10in |

Although this member of the dianthus family is a perennial, *D. barbatus*, or sweet william, gives best results when grown as a biennial. The dense flat heads of fragrant flowers range in colour from white through pink to deep cherry red. Some are marked with concentric rings of a contrasting colour. They look best grown in groups in the border, and are very popular as cut flowers.

PROPAGATION Sow seed under glass in early spring at 13°C/55°F. When large enough to handle, prick out seedlings into boxes at 7.5cm/3in apart and grow on at 10°C/50°F. Harden off and plant out in the flowering site in early summer.

GROWING A position in full sun is best, in ordinary, well-drained alkaline soil. Dress acid soils with lime before planting out.

VARIETIES There are no named varieties of sweet william, but hybrids known as 'Sweet Wivelsfield' bearing larger flower-heads have been developed.

POSSIBLE PROBLEMS Carnation ring spot causes deformed plants. Brown spots on leaves are caused by leaf spot.

GAZANIA

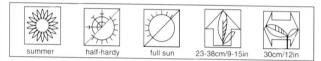

| summer | half-hardy | full sun | 23-38cm/9-15in | 30cm/12in |

Only in the very mildest areas can gazanias, natives of South Africa, be grown as perennials; elsewhere they are treated as annuals. The brilliant daisy-like flowers of cream, yellow, orange, crimson or mauve will only open in direct sunlight. The narrow leaves are grey on the underside.

PROPAGATION Sow seeds in very early spring in gentle heat. Prick seedlings into pots when they are large enough to handle. Harden off and plant out in early summer when all danger of frost is past. Tip cuttings may be taken in summer and over-wintered in the greenhouse before planting out the following year.

GROWING Gazanias must have full sun; they like well-drained soil, and do well in coastal gardens.

VARIETIES Choose from named hybrids such as 'Chansonette' (*above*), lemon, apricot, orange, carmine red; 'Sundance', large blooms, wide range of colours including cream; 'Mini Star', compact strain, yellow, gold, bronze, red.

POSSIBLE PROBLEMS Damp weather may cause grey mould.

LATHYRUS

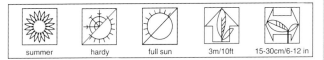

| summer | hardy | full sun | 3m/10ft | 15-30cm/6-12 in |

The sweet pea, *Lathyrus odoratus*, climbs by means of leaf tendrils. Its wing-petalled flowers are coloured white, pink, red, lilac or cream, and are sometimes strongly scented. They are extremely popular as cut flowers.

PROPAGATION Sowing can take place either in very early spring in a heated greenhouse or in late spring directly in the flowering site. To speed germination, soak the seeds in water for 12 hours before sowing. Prick out seedlings from early sowings into 7.5cm/3in pots and harden off before planting out in late spring. Plants may also be raised from summer sowings in a cold frame and set out the following year.

GROWING Sweet peas thrive on rich soil. Dig plenty of well-rotted compost or manure into the growing site before planting out. Provide pea sticks or posts and wires for support. Pinch out plants at 15cm/6in high to encourage side shoots. Pick the flowers regularly.

VARIETIES The popular Spencer group includes 'Swan Lake', white; 'Noel Sutton', deep blue; 'Leamington', lavender; 'Princess Elizabeth', coral pink and cream; 'Carlotta', carmine red. 'Knee-Hi', dwarf type, supported with light brushwood makes a bush about 1.2 x 1.2m/4 x 4ft, many colours available.

POSSIBLE PROBLEMS Slugs on leaves; mildew may occur.

NIGELLA

| summer | hardy | full sun | 15-45cm/6-18in | 23cm/9in |

Popularly known as love-in-a-mist, *Nigella damascena* is one of the group of plants typical of the English cottage garden. It looks well with lupins and aquilegias against a background of clematis and old roses. The leaves are delicate and fern-like; the flowers, usually blue but sometimes pink, resemble cornflowers.

PROPAGATION Sow seeds in the flowering site at intervals throughout the spring. Protect with cloches in colder areas. Thin out to 20cm/8in apart when the seedlings are large enough to handle. Love-in-a-mist does not transplant well.

GROWING A well-drained soil is best, and a position in full sun essential. Plants often self-seed, giving you new plants in succeeding years (though not necessarily where you would choose to put them).

VARIETIES 'Miss Jekyll', bright blue semi-double flowers; 'Persian Jewels', mixed colours – pink, red, mauve, people, blue and white.

POSSIBLE PROBLEMS Generally trouble-free.

PETUNIA

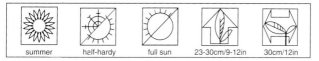

| summer | half-hardy | full sun | 23-30cm/9-12in | 30cm/12in |

Summer bedding would not be the same without the trumpet-shaped flowers of petunia hybrids providing a focus of colour that is vivid without being gaudy. Ideal for window-boxes and tubs, the trailing varieties combine particularly well with lobelia, alyssum, fuchsias and pelargoniums.

PROPAGATION Sow seed in early spring under protection with gentle heat. Prick the seedlings out into boxes when they are large enough to handle and harden off before planting out in late spring.

GROWING Petunias like reasonably fertile, free-draining soil and a warm, sunny position. Give them an occasional high-potash feed. Water regularly, especially if in containers, and remove faded flowerheads regularly. Discard after flowering.

VARIETIES Numerous named hybrids are available. Multifloras bear a profusion of 5cm/2in blooms; Grandifloras carry fewer, but larger, flowers. 'Resisto Mixed' (*above*): multi-floras, red, pink, yellow, white, blue; 'Multiflora Double Mixed', large frilled flowers; 'Super Fanfare Mixed', grandiflo-ras, double flowers.

POSSIBLE PROBLEMS Aphids on young shoots.

27

RUDBECKIA

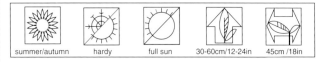

| summer/autumn | hardy | full sun | 30-60cm/12-24in | 45cm /18in |

Rudbeckia hirta, the original Black-eyed Susan, is treated as an annual, though strictly it is a perennial like its relatives *R. laciniata* (the coneflower) and *R. nitida*. Its bright yellow or orange flowers with contrasting dark centres are eye-catching candidates for the border and make good cut flowers.

PROPAGATION Sow seed in early spring in trays in a cold frame or greenhouse. Prick out the seedlings when large enough to handle and plant into the flowering site.

GROWING Annual rudbeckias like a dry, free-draining soil, unlike the perennials which prefer heavy, moisture-retentive loam. They tolerate dappled shade but prefer a sunny position. In the open, support the plants with stakes.

VARIETIES 'Marmalade' bears orange flowers up to 7.5 cm/ 3in across; 'Rustic Dwarfs' (*above*) are of equal size in shades of orange and bronze.

POSSIBLE PROBLEMS Generally trouble-free.

TAGETES

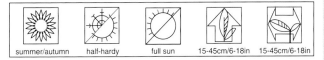

| summer/autumn | half-hardy | full sun | 15-45cm/6-18in | 15-45cm/6-18in |

Tagetes patula, the French marigold, is in fact a native of Mexico. Various strains produce flowers of yellow and orange, sometimes blotched with crimson or bronze, some with double flowers. Very long-lived, they add a bright note to the border and make good cut flowers.

PROPAGATION Sow seeds under protection in early spring and prick the seedlings out into boxes when they are large enough to handle. Harden off before planting out in late spring. Pinch out any premature flowerbuds. Seeds may be sown directly into the flowering site in late spring.

GROWING Marigolds are not fussy about soil, but like a sunny, open site. Dead-head regularly to encourage continued flowering. Discard at the end of the season.

VARIETIES Of the many good named varieties, try 'Naughty Marietta', yellow, blotched maroon; 'Monarch Mixed', compact double flowers ranging in colour from yellow to deep mahogany; 'Queen Sophia' syn. 'Scarlet Sophia', double flowers, russet-red laced with gold. *T. patula* is crossed with *T. erecta* to give Afro-French hybrids such as 'Suzie Wong' which are compact and early flowering.

POSSIBLE PROBLEMS Damp conditions cause grey mould.

ALTHAEA

| summer | hardy | semi-shade | 2.4m/8ft | 90cm/3ft |

Althaea rosea (above), the familiar hollyhock, is well suited to cottage gardens and because of its great height looks impressive at the back of an informal border, particularly when a fine old wall provides protection. The showy, trumpet-shaped flowers of the species are in shades of pink, but named varieties are available in red, cream and white.

GROWING Hollyhocks do best if treated as biennials. Set out young plants in autumn in any ordinary soil, in a sheltered site. Strong stakes should be provided from early spring. On light soils, apply a moisture-retaining mulch in hot weather. For perennial growth, cut back plants after flowering to 15cm/6in; otherwise discard the plants.

PROPAGATION Sow seed in trays of compost in early spring. Prick the seedlings out into 7.5cm/3in pots when they are large enough to handle and plant out in late summer for flowering the following year.

VARIETIES 'Chater's Double', peony-like double flowers, all colours; 'Begonia Flowered Crested', mixed colours.

POSSIBLE PROBLEMS Caterpillars damage the stems and leaves. Rust is more likely on plants treated as perennials and can be severe.

ASTILBE

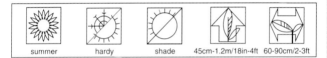

summer	hardy	shade	45cm-1.2m/18in-4ft	60-90cm/2-3ft

Astilbe species come from China and Japan. From these the garden hybrid *A.* × *arendsii* (*above*) has been developed to display the best qualities of the family. They are bushy, erect plants, forming impressive clumps of fern-like leaves; the taller types are most effective for ground cover. Feathery plumes of pink or white flowers are carried on delicate stems. They make excellent waterside plants.

GROWING Plant from autumn to spring in moist soil in a cool, shady position (although a sunny site is acceptable if the soil is never allowed to dry out). Astilbes dislike chalky soil. Water well in dry weather and apply an annual moisture-retaining mulch such as leaf mould, well-rotted compost or manure in early spring. Do not cut the plants back until the end of winter, as the faded flowerheads and foliage are attractive in their own right.

PROPAGATION Divide woody clumps in spring, ensuring that each portion has 2-3 developing buds.

VARIETIES 'Fanal', 60cm/24in, red; 'Bressingham Beauty', 90cm/3ft, rose-pink; 'Deutschland', 60cm/24in, brilliant white.

POSSIBLE PROBLEMS Generally trouble-free.

CAMPANULA

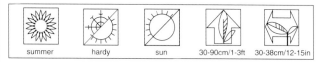

| summer | hardy | sun | 30-90cm/1-3ft | 30-38cm/12-15in |

The bellflower family includes a great number of attractive species including *Campanula medium*, the well-loved biennial Canterbury bell, and several exquisite alpine plants. For the border, *C. persicifolia*, the peach-leaved campanula, is an excellent choice with its impressive height, breathtaking flowers and evergreen foliage. *C. Lactiflora* (*above*) bears pale, lavender-blue, bell-shaped flowers in early and mid summer.

GROWING Set out young plants in autumn in well-drained fertile soil; chalky soils are tolerated. A sunny site is preferred but light shade will do no great harm. Stake the plants when they reach 15cm/6in high.

PROPAGATION Divide established clumps in autumn. *C. persicifolia* does not come true from seed.

VARIETIES *C. persicifolia* 'Telham Beauty', deep, rich blue; 'Planiflora' (syn. *C. nitida*), dwarf at 23-30cm/9-12in, blue flowers; 'Planiflora Alba' is a white form.

POSSIBLE PROBLEMS Slugs and snails may damage leaves and shoots. Leaf spot fungus and rust may damage leaves.

CONVALLARIA

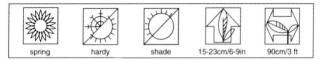

| spring | hardy | shade | 15-23cm/6-9in | 90cm/3 ft |

The lily-of-the-valley, *Convallaria majalis (above)*, is one of the prettiest spring flowers, its graceful stems clothed with pure white bell-shaped blooms. With handsome leaves, it makes excellent ground cover in shady spots, spreading by means of creeping rhizomes. The lightly fragrant flowers are popular with flower arrangers.

GROWING Start with 'pips' (root pieces with buds). Plant in autumn 5cm/2in deep in heavy, moisture-retentive soil that has previously been enriched with plenty of well-rotted organic matter. Mulch with leaf mould every autumn.

PROPAGATION Lift the rhizomes between autumn and spring and separate into crowns; replant, just covering with soil, and dress with leaf mould. Water well.

VARIETIES 'Fortin's Giant', white; 'Rosea', pink; 'Variegata', leaves striped with gold.

POSSIBLE PROBLEMS Caterpillars damage the rhizomes; grey mould on leaves in wet weather.

COREOPSIS

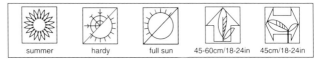

| summer | hardy | full sun | 45-60cm/18-24in | 45cm/18-24in |

Native to North America, the coreopsis is an accommodating plant, producing cheerful yellow star-shaped flowers throughout the summer even in polluted atmospheres.

GROWING Set out young plants between autumn and spring in well-drained, fertile soil. Chalky soils are tolerated. A position in full sun in an open border is preferred. Cut back some stems in late summer to encourage perennial growth.

PROPAGATION Divide established plants in early autumn or very early spring, making sure that each portion has 4-5 new shoots. Replant immediately. *C. grandiflora* can be increased by 7.5cm/3in basal cuttings taken in summer and rooted in a cold frame.

SPECIES *C. verticillata* (*above*), very fine leaves, a succession of star-shaped flowers 2.5cm/1in wide from mid to late summer; *C. grandiflora*, a short-lived perennial, up to 90cm/3ft high, bearing large daisy-like flowers all summer. This is the best species for cutting; named varieties include 'Mayfield Giant', 'Sunray', double flowers, and 'Goldfink', dwarf at 23cm/9in.

POSSIBLE PROBLEMS Froghoppers damage young shoots.

DELPHINIUM

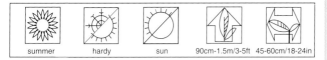

| summer | hardy | sun | 90cm-1.5m/3-5ft | 45-60cm/18-24in |

Delphiniums are unquestionably the most magnificent flowers in the herbaceous border. Quite apart from their great height, the profusion of blooms and intensity of colour – usually blue, but sometimes pink or cream – make an unforgettable impression. Most garden types are hybrids bred from *D. elatum* and other species, giving two strains known as Elatum or Large-flowered (up to 2.4m/8ft, and including the Pacific hybrids, *above*) and Belladonna (about 1.2m/4ft).

GROWING Set out young plants from autumn to spring in deep, rich soil on a sheltered site. Provide stout canes for support. Cut back to ground level after flowering.

PROPAGATION Divide established plants in spring or take 7.5cm/3in basal cuttings and insert in a peat/sand mixture in a cold frame. Transfer to a nursery bed when rooted and grow on until planting out in autumn.

VARIETIES The choice is wide. 'Blue Jade', Pacific, dwarf at 1.2m/4ft, sky-blue; 'Wendy', Belladonna, gentian blue; 'Butterball', Elatum, rich cream.

POSSIBLE PROBLEMS Slugs and snails damage young shoots.

35

GERANIUM

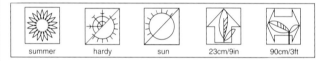

| summer | hardy | sun | 23cm/9in | 90cm/3ft |

Geraniums, popularly known as cranesbills, comprise a large family of flowering plants, including some alpine species. All summer and into the autumn, they bear open, five-petalled flowers about 25cm/1in or more across, in shades of pink, crimson, blue and white. The leaves are rounded, sometimes deeply cut; the plants form large round clumps that look attractive in the summer border or any informal planting scheme.

GROWING Set out young plants between autumn and spring in any type of well-drained soil. Do not let them dry out in hot weather.

PROPAGATION Divide and replant established clumps in autumn or spring.

SPECIES *G. endressii* reaches 40cm/16in in height and spreads to 60cm/24in or more. Named varieties include 'A.T. Johnson', silvery pink, and 'Rose Clair', white edged purple. The hybrid G. × 'Claridge Druce', with deep mauve blooms, makes excellent ground cover. *G. sanguineum* (*above*) is low-growing, mat-forming, with magenta flowers; *G. s. lancastrense* is a great favourite with pale pink flowers veined with red.

POSSIBLE PROBLEMS Slugs may eat young plants.

Helleborus

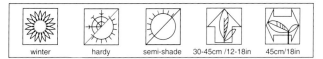

| winter | hardy | semi-shade | 30-45cm /12-18in | 45cm/18in |

No gardener who wants to enjoy flowers all the year round can afford to ignore the Christmas rose, *Helleborus niger*, which produces its exquisite white blooms in deepest winter. The Lenten rose, *H. orientalis*, is equally valuable, blooming from winter into early spring with dramatically coloured flowers of green, white, pink, red-purple or black-purple, often splashed inside with a contrasting colour. As cut flowers hellebores are very long-lasting.

GROWING Set out young plants in small groups in autumn in deep, moisture-retentive but well-drained soil into which plenty of well-rotted compost or leaf mould has been incorporated. Choose a site where they can be left for years: they dislike disturbance. Protect the flowers of the Christmas rose as they open with cloches. Cut stems right back after flowering; apply an annual mulch in the autumn.

PROPAGATION Divide well-established plants in spring and replant immediately. Alternatively sow seeds in sandy soil in a cold frame in summer. Prick off the seedlings into a nursery bed and grow on until planting out in the autumn of the following year. They will not flower for 2-3 years.

VARIETIES *H. niger* 'Potter's Wheel' (*above*), exceptional white form.

POSSIBLE PROBLEMS Leaf spot.

37

HEMEROCALLIS

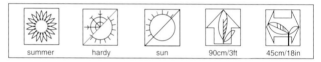

| summer | hardy | sun | 90cm/3ft | 45cm/18in |

Three species of the hemerocallis are available, but much more popular are hybrids which can be found in dozens of different colours. The common name, day lily, refers to the fact that each flower lives for one day only, to be replaced by another the next morning. This process continues for 6-8 weeks; by choosing a mixture of varieties it is possible to have a display of these fabulous blooms for the entire summer.

GROWING Plant between autumn and spring in moist, rich soil. Full sun is preferred but a little shade is tolerated. Remove dead stems and leaves in late autumn.

PROPAGATION Divide established clumps in early autumn or spring just as young growth starts. Seeds do not come true to type.

VARIETIES 'Golden Chimes' (*above*); 'Chartreuse Magic', sharp yellow and green; 'Morocco Red', dusky red and yellow; 'Pink Damask', pink with yellow throat.

POSSIBLE PROBLEMS Generally trouble-free.

PERENNIALS

IMPATIENS

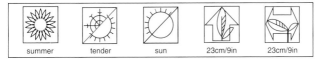

| summer | tender | sun | 23cm/9in | 23cm/9in |

Familiar even to non-gardeners, *Impatiens walleriana* or busy lizzie is a short-lived perennial native to Africa. Usually grown indoors or in a greenhouse, dwarf hybrids between *I. walleriana* and *I. sultanii* can be used in outdoor bedding schemes and are ideal for tubs and windowboxes. They are admired for their dense foliage and five-petalled flowers of red, pink or white which appear throughout the summer.

GROWING Set young plants out in early summer in well-drained soil in a sheltered position. Pinch out the growing tips to promote bushy growth. Dead-head regularly.

PROPAGATION Sow seed in pans in spring at 16-18°C/61-64°F. Prick the seedlings off into boxes when they are large enough to handle, then into individual 7.5cm/3in pots of compost. Harden off before planting out.

VARIETIES The Imp strain (*above*) includes varieties in white, shocking pink, carmine, scarlet and purple; 'Tangleglow', orange; 'Zig Zag', striped.

POSSIBLE PROBLEMS Aphids infest leaves and stems. Slugs may damage seedlings.

L UPIN

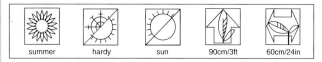

| summer | hardy | sun | 90cm/3ft | 60cm/24in |

Lupins are traditionally a feature of informal cottage gardens, but their tall spires in a range of soft colours make a striking contribution to the border in any garden design. The most reliable types are hybrids of the species *L. polyphyllus*.

GROWING Set out young plants in early spring or in the autumn, in light, slightly acid soil. Neutral soils will do, but lupins hate lime, and in heavy soils the stems become too soft to support the flowers. Stake with twiggy sticks when plants are 15cm/6in high. Wait until late winter before cutting back, to prevent water lodging in the hollow stems.

PROPAGATION Take 7.5cm/3in cuttings, with a little rootstock attached, in spring. Insert in sandy soil in a cold frame; pot on when rooted or set in nursery rows before planting out in the autumn. Named varieties do not come true from seed.

VARIETIES Choose forms of the Russell lupin strain. Many are bi-coloured. 'Blushing Bride', cream and white; 'Cherry Pie', crimson and yellow; 'Jane Eyre', violet and white; 'Lilac Time', rose-lilac and white; 'Limelight', butter yellow; 'Guardsman', vermilion.

POSSIBLE PROBLEMS Crown rot, root rot, honey fungus.

MALVA

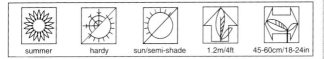

| summer | hardy | sun/semi-shade | 1.2m/4ft | 45-60cm/18-24in |

The mallow, *Malva alcea*, is a tall, bushy plant particularly useful on poor soils. It bears abundant mauve trumpet-shaped flowers all summer.

GROWING Plant from autumn to spring on light, well-drained soil in sun or partial shade. Provide twiggy sticks for support. Cut down dead stems in late autumn or winter.

PROPAGATION Take 7.5cm/3in basal cuttings in late spring. Insert in sandy soil in a cold frame and transfer to the flowering site in autumn. Plants may be raised from seed sown under protection with gentle warmth in spring. Prick the seedlings out into a nursery bed when they are large enough to handle and grow on until transferring to the flowering site in the autumn.

VARIETIES *M. alcea* 'Fastigiata' (*above*) is more upright than the species and reaches only 90cm/3ft.

POSSIBLE PROBLEMS Rust may affect the leaves and stems.

Meconopsis

| summer | hardy | semi-shade | 60cm/24in | 30cm/12in |

Meconopsis bear showy, poppy-like flowers in spring and summer on slender stems above neat rosettes of attractive leaves. They are beautiful plants for a mixed border.

GROWING A free-draining but moisture-retentive soil is essential, preferably non-alkaline. Meconopsis like a position in semi-shade and sheltered from wind. Water well in summer and support with pea sticks. Clear away old seedheads and foliage in late summer.

PROPAGATION Collect ripe seed from the plants in late summer and sow in a cold frame. Transfer the seedlings to boxes and keep over winter in a cold frame. Transplant to nursery rows until planting in the permanent site in the autumn.

SPECIES *M. cambrica* (Welsh poppy, *above*), vivid golden flowers in summer, self-seeds very freely, does not withstand hot summers; *M. betonicifolia* (Tibetan poppy), up to 90cm/3ft high, large, deep blue flowers in early summer, best choice for higher temperatures; *M. napaulensis*, up to 2m/6½ft high, with beautiful leaves and large blue, purple, red or pink flowers in early summer.

POSSIBLE PROBLEMS Downy mildew, black bean aphid.

Oenothera

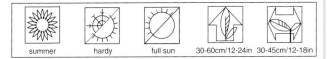

| summer | hardy | full sun | 30-60cm/12-24in | 30-45cm/12-18in |

The oenothera family of North America includes the evening primrose, *O. biennis*. Most species bear yellow flowers, though some are white. Lightly scented, they are funnel-shaped at first but open almost flat. They bring prolonged and brilliant colour to the border, and because they self-seed freely are also good for wild gardens.

GROWING Set out small groups of young plants in the autumn, on light, free-draining soil. Oenotheras like an open, sunny site but will tolerate light shade. Water well in dry weather and dead-head regularly unless you want plants to self-seed. Cut down the stems after flowering.

PROPAGATION Divide established plants between autumn and spring. These perennials are short-lived but self-seed freely and successfully.

SPECIES *O. perennis*, syn. *O. pumila*, small, yellow flowers, pale green leaves, mid-summer; *O. missouriensis*, suitable for rock gardens or the front of the border at 15cm/6in high, abundant yellow flowers all summer; *O. fruticosa*, the variety 'Yellow River' bears a profusion of deep golden yellow flowers, mid-summer; *O. tetragona* 'Fireworks' (*above*) bears yellow flowers throughout the summer.

POSSIBLE PROBLEMS Heavy, waterlogged soil encourages root rot.

43

PAEONIA

spring/summer	hardy	sun/semi-shade	60-90cm/2-3ft	45-60cm/18-24in

Peonies have an exotic air, with huge, bowl-shaped flowers that open in late spring or early summer. Large, handsome leaves set off to perfection the blooms of white, yellow, pink or red, some of which are double, some fragrant.

GROWING Peonies like moisture-retentive, well-drained soil, in sun or partial shade; choose a site that is sheltered from early morning sun. Before planting, dig the ground to a spade's depth, incorporating plenty of well-rotted organic matter. Set out young plants in suitable weather between autumn and spring, with the crowns just 2.5cm/1in below the soil surface. On light soil especially, mulch each spring with well-rotted compost. Peonies resent disturbance – choose a site where they can be left alone. Dead-head regularly. Cut back foliage in autumn.

PROPAGATION Divide and replant in early autumn, cutting the crowns with a sharp knife.

VARIETIES *Paeonia lactiflora* hybrids: 'Whitleyi Major', white, single flowers, golden stamens; 'The Moor', deep crimson, single; 'Felix Crousse', rose-red, double. *P. officinalis*: 'Alba Plena' (*above*): double, white; 'Rubra Plena', double, deep red.

POSSIBLE PROBLEMS Peony blight; leaf spot.

PAPAVER

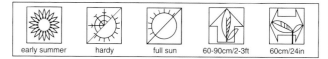

| early summer | hardy | full sun | 60-90cm/2-3ft | 60cm/24in |

The oriental poppy, *Papaver orientale (above)*, is an eye-catching border plant bearing vivid but short-lived scarlet flowers up to 10cm/4 in across. Cultivated varieties extend the colour range to pink, crimson and white.

GROWING Set out young plants in small groups in autumn or early spring in free-draining soil in a sunny, open site sheltered from wind. Provide supporting canes for the growing plants. Cut back to ground level after flowering.

PROPAGATION Divide established plants in early spring and replant immediately. Alternatively, take root cuttings in winter and insert in a cold frame. Transfer to 7.5cm/3in pots of compost when 3 or 4 pairs of leaves have appeared. Stand outdoors in summer and set out in the autumn in the permanent site. Plants may also be raised from seed sown in spring in the greenhouse.

VARIETIES 'Black and White', white flowers, black centre; 'Perry's White'; 'King George', scarlet, frilled petals; 'Mrs Perry', soft coral; 'Enchantress', carmine.

POSSIBLE PROBLEMS Downy mildew on leaves.

PELARGONIUM

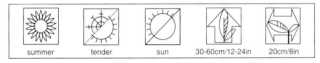

| summer | tender | sun | 30-60cm/12-24in | 20cm/8in |

Pelargoniums are often (wrongly) called geraniums, the name properly given to the hardy perennial cranesbill. Native to Africa, these tender species with their showy blooms are an essential element in hanging baskets, window boxes and tubs as well as summer bedding schemes. Among the most popular types for this purpose are the hybrids known as Regal and Zonal pelargoniums, which are available in all shades of pink, red, maroon and white. Zonal hybrids have beautifully coloured leaves.

GROWING Set out young plants in early summer in moderately fertile soil in full sun. Remove faded flowerheads. Water freely, giving a high-potash feed occasionally. In autumn put plants under protection. Cut back older plants and put up in good compost.

PROPAGATION Take cuttings from overwintered plants in spring and insert in a peat/sand mixture. Pot on when rooted. Plants may also be raised successfully from seed sown under protection in early spring.

VARIETIES 'Princess of Wales', frilled, strawberry pink; 'Grand Slam' (*above*), abundant rose-red blooms; 'Nomad', white, blotched pink. Many other good varieties.

POSSIBLE PROBLEMS Low night temperatures cause reddening of leaves and stems. Leaves turn yellow if soil is too dry.

POLYANTHUS

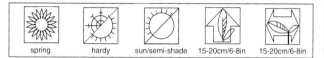

| spring | hardy | sun/semi-shade | 15-20cm/6-8in | 15-20cm/6-8in |

The primula family comprises a number of hardy perennials including *Primula veris*, the cowslip, and *P. vulgaris*, the primrose. The polyanthus is a hybrid of these two, with characteristic whorls of primrose flowers in a huge variety of colours, carried on strong stems above a rosette of oval leaves. They can be treated as indoor pot plants, but are ideal at the front of the border or in tubs and window boxes.

GROWING Set out plants in autumn or spring in heavy, moist soil into which plenty of organic matter has been incorporated. A site in full sun or partial shade will do.

PROPAGATION Divide the plants every 3 years immediately after flowering and replant straight away.

VARIETIES Pacific strain (*above*), large blooms, early flowering, bright colours including white, yellow, pink, red, purple and blue; 'Cowichan', mixed colours, no central eye.

POSSIBLE PROBLEMS Slugs on leaves in spring; grey mould; leaf spot on older plants.

PULMONARIA

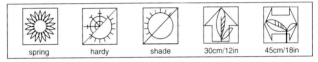

| spring | hardy | shade | 30cm/12in | 45cm/18in |

Pulmonarias are ideal plants for a shady part of the garden, where they will spread their handsome oval leaves to make dense ground cover. In early spring clusters of drooping bell-shaped flowers appear, held clear of the foliage on erect stems. The blooms are pink, often turning blue later.

GROWING Set out young plants in autumn or spring in reasonably moist fertile soil. Apply an annual mulch of peat in spring and water well during the growing period. Remove dead leaves in the autumn.

PROPAGATION Divide established clumps in autumn or spring.

SPECIES *P. angustifolia* (blue cowslip), height 23cm/9in, dark green leaves, spring-flowering; *P. officinalis* (Jerusalem cowslip), height 23-30cm/9-12in, light green leaves blotched silver, late spring-flowering; *P. saccharata* (*above*), 30cm/12in, pointed leaves beautifully marked cream, late spring-flowering; the variety 'White Wings' bears white flowers.

POSSIBLE PROBLEMS Slugs may eat young shoots.

TROLLIUS

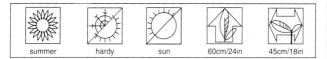

| summer | hardy | sun | 60cm/24in | 45cm/18in |

There are several species of trollius, the globe flower, in cultivation, all bearing impressive rounded blooms in various shades of yellow with prominent stamens. They are ideal for waterside planting or in the border, coming into flower in late spring and again in late summer if the stems are cut right back after flowering.

GROWING Plant out in autumn or spring in rather heavy, moisture-retentive soil. Keep well-watered, especially in hot dry spells. Some shade is tolerated.

PROPAGATION Divide the fibrous rootstock in autumn and replant immediately.

SPECIES *Trollius ledebourii* (*above*), bright, orange-yellow, cup-shaped flowers; *T. × cultorum*, garden hybrid, only 30-45cm/12-18in high. Good varieties are 'Earliest of All', clear yellow; 'Salamander', reddish orange; 'Canary Bird', pale yellow.

POSSIBLE PROBLEMS Smut causes swellings on leaves and stems.

TROPAEOLUM

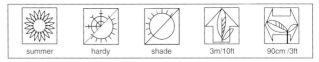

| summer | hardy | shade | 3m/10ft | 90cm /3ft |

Tropaeolums include the familiar garden nasturtium, *T. majus*, and the canary creeper, *T. peregrinum*, both annuals, which climb by twisting their leaf stalks around any available support. *T. speciosum* (*above*), or flame nasturtium, is a rhizomatous perennial which bears bright red flowers on slender stems from mid to late summer. Attractive green leaves echo the radiating form of the petals. There are no named varieties of the species.

GROWING Despite its South American origin, the flame nasturtium does not like full sun – a shaded wall is ideal. Set out plants in spring in fertile, slightly acid soil, if necessary adding peat. Supports are essential, but a leafy shrub will serve this purpose as well as wires or canes.

PROPAGATION Divide the rhizomes in spring.

POSSIBLE PROBLEMS Aphids may infest the stems.

VIOLA

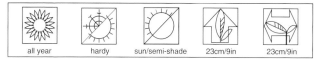

all year	hardy	sun/semi-shade	23cm/9in	23cm/9in

Garden pansies, *Viola × wittrockiana*, are short-lived perennial hybrids. They are among the most popular of all cultivated plants, with their large, colourful flowers, bushy foliage and easy-going nature. The colour range is huge and different varieties are in bloom almost all year.

GROWING Time of planting depends on variety. Set out in moisture-retentive but well-drained soil. Add peat and/or leaf mould to chalky soils. Snip off faded flowers to ensure a succession of blooms.

PROPAGATION Divide mature plants in early spring or take 5cm/2in cuttings of non-flowering basal shoots in summer and insert in a peat/sand mixture in a cold frame. Pot on when rooted and plant out in autumn or spring.

VARIETIES Countless varieties are available, in single colours – white, yellow, apricot, red, violet and blue – and numerous combinations, often with a black blotch.

POSSIBLE PROBLEMS Leaf spot; fungi of different kinds cause pansy sickness.

COLCHICUM

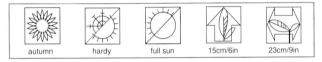

| autumn | hardy | full sun | 15cm/6in | 23cm/9in |

The autumn crocus is not in fact related to the crocus, though they look similar when in flower. Colchicums are members of the lily family (crocuses belong to the iris family), with oval (not flat) corms and long, rather untidy leaves. This feature should be borne in mind when choosing a planting site, as the leaves persist long after the flowers have died down. As they can be left undisturbed for years, it is a good idea to group them in rough grass.

GROWING Plant the corms in late summer in any type of well-drained soil. Set them 10cm/4in deep in small groups. Lift and divide when overcrowded.

PROPAGATION Lift the corms in summer, detach the offsets and replant immediately.

SPECIES *C. speciosum (above)*, flowers in shades of mauve. Beautiful hybrids developed from the species include 'The Giant', large mauve flowers, white centre; 'Album', pure white; 'Atrorubens', crimson-purple.

POSSIBLE PROBLEMS Slugs may eat the corms and leaves.

CROCUS

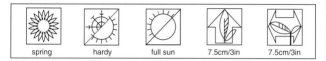

| spring | hardy | full sun | 7.5cm/3in | 7.5cm/3in |

The sight of budding crocuses is welcomed as a signal of spring. In fact these hardy plants, grown from corms, flower from late summer until spring, according to species. Colours include blue, purple, white, yellow and mauve. Some varieties are striped; many have vivid golden stamens. Very low-growing, with cup-shaped flowers rising directly from the ground, crocuses do well in rock gardens, troughs and at the edge of a border. Winter and early spring-flowering types can be used in lawns.

GROWING Plant in autumn in well-drained soil, preferably in groups, in a sunny position with protection from wind. Do not dead-head; leave the foliage until it is yellow and can be pulled off easily.

PROPAGATION Take offsets after flowering. Replant the larger cormlets for flowering the following year. The smaller ones can be grown on in drills until they reach flowering size.

SPECIES Try hybrids of *Crocus chrysanthus* such as 'E. P. Bowles', butter yellow, spring-flowering; *C. longiflorus* is scented, autumn-flowering, deep purple; spring-flowering Dutch crocuses deriving from *C. vernus* include 'Joan of Arc', white and 'Queen of the Blues', with large, lavender flowers. *C. imperati*, lilac streaked purple, blooms in mid-winter.

POSSIBLE PROBLEMS Mice and birds may damage the corms.

CYCLAMEN

| summer | hardy | semi-shade | 10cm/4in | 10-15cm/4-6in |

Hardy cyclamens are cousins of the familiar flowering house-plant *Cyclamen persicum*. They are diminutive but charming plants and once established they flower for years. The beautifully marked foliage makes long-lasting ground cover in shady corners. *C. neapolitanum (above)* is the best species for this purpose, with flowers in various shades of pink appearing from late summer to late autumn. The deep green leaves are variable in shape – the alternative name, *C. hederifolium*, reflects their occasional resemblance to ivy – but are always streaked silver, and red on the underside.

GROWING Plant the tubers in late summer/early autumn in clusters barely covered with soil. Well-drained soil containing plenty of well-rotted organic matter is best. Choose a shady site sheltered from wind. Mulch annually with a 2.5cm/1in layer of leaf mould when the foliage has died down.

PROPAGATION As offsets are not produced, cyclamens must be increased from seed. Collect ripe seed in summer and sow in early autumn in pots of seed compost kept in a ventilated cold frame. Prick the seedlings out into small pots of potting compost. Overwinter in a cold frame and plant out in late spring.

VARIETIES *C. n.* 'Album' is a white form.

POSSIBLE PROBLEMS Generally trouble-free.

DAHLIA

| summer | half-hardy | sun/semi-shade | 45cm/18in | 45-60cm/18-24in |

When dahlias are grown for exhibition purposes, a process of disbudding is carried out to produce fewer, larger flowers. This is not necessary in normal circumstances, but it is advisable to pinch out the leading shoots once, a month after planting. Lift and store the tubers annually. Raise them carefully, using a spade, a week after frost has turned the leaves black. Drain off water from the stems. Store healthy tubers only. Place them in boxes, just covered with peat, in a frostproof place. Inspect from time to time to make sure none is affected by mould.

PROPAGATION Set overwintered tubers in boxes of peat and sand in spring, with the crowns visible. Keep moist and frost-free. When the 'eyes' begin to swell, cut the tubers into pieces, each with an eye, and pot up or plant 10cm/4in deep in a cold frame. Plant out when danger of frost is passed.

VARIETIES Single: 'Sion', bronze; Anemone: 'Lucy', purple, yellow centre; Collerette: 'Can-Can', pink, yellow inner ring; Decorative: 'Little Tiger', red and cream, dwarf; Ball: 'Gloire de Lyon', white; Pompon: 'Nero', maroon; Cactus: 'Bach', yellow.

POSSIBLE PROBLEMS Aphids, caterpillars, earwigs; grey mould, petal blight.

GALANTHUS

| spring | hardy | semi-shade | 7.5cm/3in | 10cm/4in |

No garden is complete without snowdrops, one of the first bulbs to flower outdoors. There are several varieties. *Galanthus nivalis* (*above*) is the common snowdrop, with nodding white flowers dotted green, the best for naturalizing in grass or beneath shrubs. Large-flowered varieties are a better choice for the open ground.

GROWING Plant the fresh bulbs as soon as they are available: snowdrops can be difficult to establish and the bulbs must not dry out. Set them in moisture-retentive loam in a position where they will receive good light in very early spring.

PROPAGATION Once established, snowdrops multiply freely. Lift and divide the clusters while in flower or just afterwards and replant immediately. Separate each bulb carefully so that its leaves and roots are undamaged. Plants may be raised from seed – in fact thriving plants may self-seed – and take 5 years to reach maturity.

SPECIES *G. nivalis reginae-olgae*, sub-species, flowers in autumn before the leaves appear; *G. n.* 'Flore-Plena', double, showy flowers; *G. n.* 'Viridapicis', large flowers, green spot on both outer and inner petals; *G. elwesii*, up to 25cm/10in high, spring-flowering, green inner petals.

POSSIBLE PROBLEMS Bulb eelworm; narcissus fly maggots; grey mould on leaves.

GLADIOLUS

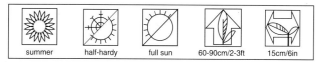

| summer | half-hardy | full sun | 60-90cm/2-3ft | 15cm/6in |

Gladioli bear their lily-like flowers on one side of an erect spike. Large-flowered hybrids are the best choice for the garden border; for cutting, choose Primulinus hybrids, 45-90cm/18in-3ft high, or Miniatures, the same height but with numerous smaller florets. The colour range is breathtaking, including both bright and subtle shades, but no blues.

GROWING Dig a layer of well-rotted manure into the site in early spring. Rake bonemeal into the surface at 75g/m^2 (3oz/sq. yd). Plant corms 10cm/4in deep, more in light soil, in spring. If the corms are not deep enough the mature plants may keel over. Space gladioli for cutting in rows 30cm/12in apart. Keep weed-free. Do not water for 8-10 weeks, then water generously. When the foliage yellows lift the corms and cut off the main stem to 1cm/ ½in. Dry off in warmth and store in a cool frost-free place.

PROPAGATION Detach cormlets from the base of the parent and treat in the same way, raising them in nursery beds and storing over winter until they reach flowering size in the second year.

VARIETIES Large-flowered: 'Peter Pears' *(above)*, salmon pink; Primulinus: 'Apex', warm red; Miniature: 'Greenbird', sulphur green.

POSSIBLE PROBLEMS Thrips, soil pests, gladiolus dry rot.

Hyacinthus

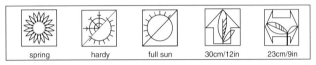

| spring | hardy | full sun | 30cm/12in | 23cm/9in |

The hyacinth bears spikes of fragrant flowers of white, blue, yellow, pink or red in early spring. Most of the generally available varieties belong to the group called Dutch hybrids, developed from the species *Hyacinthus orientalis*. They are commercially forced into flowering early for indoor plants, but are ideal for spring flowering outdoors in more formal schemes.

GROWING Plant the bulbs as soon as they are available in early autumn, in rich, well-drained soil. A sunny site is important if you want the bulbs to bloom for more than one year.

PROPAGATION Hyacinths are not prolific, but offsets can be taken from the parent bulb, which should be lifted after the foliage has died down. Replant the bulbils immediately.

VARIETIES Recommended for bedding: 'King of the Blues', deep blue; 'La Victoire', red; 'Pink Pearl' (*above*), deep pink; 'L'Innocence', white; 'City of Haarlem', primrose yellow.

POSSIBLE PROBLEMS Stem and bulb eelworm; narcissus fly maggots.

IRIS BULBS

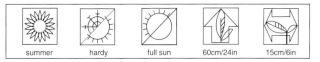

| summer | hardy | full sun | 60cm/24in | 15cm/6in |

Bulbous irises are a small group which include the dwarf reticulated types ideal for rockeries and pot culture. For general garden cultivation hybrids of the xiphium group are best. These fall into three categories: Dutch irises are first to flower in early summer; the Spanish irises bloom about 2 weeks later, and finally the English irises 2 weeks later still. All come in a range of delectable colours, but the English group, while it bears flowers 12.5cm/5in across, contains no yellows.

GROWING Plant the bulbs in autumn 10-15cm/4-6in deep, in light, fertile soil in the case of Dutch and Spanish hybrids. The English hybrids like rich, damp soil.

PROPAGATION Lift the bulbs after flowering. Detach the offsets and replant immediately, placing the smallest specimens in a nursery bed for a year.

VARIETIES Dutch: 'Golden Harvest', vivid yellow; 'National Velvet', deep purple, blotched orange. Spanish: 'Frederika', white blotched yellow; 'Blue River', aquamarine blotched orange. English: 'Prince Albert', silvery blue; 'Mirabeau', purple blotched white.

POSSIBLE PROBLEMS Narcissus fly larvae; grey bulb rot.

LILIUM SPECIES

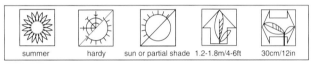

summer	hardy	sun or partial shade	1.2-1.8m/4-6ft	30cm/12in

In spite of its majestic, exotic appearance, the lily is generally not difficult to grow. The numerous species and hybrids are divided into 9 groups according to origin, with true species in Division 9. All lily bulbs, made up of tightly packed scales, produce roots from the base, but some also have roots from the stems; this type should be planted deeper than basal-rooting bulbs. Flowers may be trumpet-shaped, bowl-shaped or, in the form called Turk's-cap, with recurved petals. The colour range is very wide, excluding blue.

GROWING Plant fresh bulbs from autumn to spring (basal rooting bulbs always in autumn), about 15cm/6in deep depending on size. A south-facing site sheltered from wind is best; ordinary well-drained soil will do. While some species dislike lime, others prefer it. Enrich soil with well-rotted organic matter before planting.

PROPAGATION Some lilies produce numerous offsets which may be treated in the usual way. Scale propagation is suitable for all types.

SPECIES *Lilium regale* (*above*), China, fragrant, white, trumpet flowers 15cm/6in long, stem-rooting bulbs which increase quickly; *L. pardalinum* (panther lily), California, 5cm/2in orange-red Turk's-cap flowers, basal rooting bulb, needs lime-free soil.

POSSIBLE PROBLEMS Leatherjackets; lily beetle larvae.

Narcissus Species

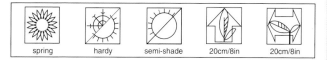

| spring | hardy | semi-shade | 20cm/8in | 20cm/8in |

Species of wild daffodils are generally smaller than the cultivated hybrids and the flower form is very varied. Most do well in the open, left alone to flower for many years. Some are good for rock gardens. Varieties suitable for naturalizing in grass, for which narcissi are perhaps the ideal subject, are described below.

GROWING Naturalized narcissi do best in rich soil, protected by the shade of larger plants such as trees and shrubs. Soil should not be waterlogged or too dry. Plant in late summer with random spacing; scatter the bulbs on the ground and plant them where they fall, in holes three times the depth of the bulb.

PROPAGATION If necessary, lift and divide the bulbs after flowering and replant immediately.

SPECIES *Narcissus cyclamineus* 'February Gold' *(above)*, early-flowering species with rich yellow, swept-back flowers; in moist soil it will seed and increase freely; best in fine grass. *N. pseudonarcissus*, the wild daffodil or lent lily, up to 30cm/12in high, creamy petals with lemon trumpets; the better choice for tall grass.

POSSIBLE PROBLEMS Given suitable conditions, naturalized narcissi are relatively trouble-free.

TULIPA

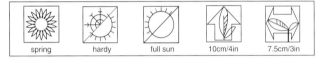

| spring | hardy | full sun | 10cm/4in | 7.5cm/3in |

Tulips were introduced to Europe from Turkey in the 16th century and have been firm favourites ever since. Most of the cultivated forms now seen are hybrids classified into 14 divisions according to their characteristics. Division 15 comprises the exquisite species tulips, many of which are ideal for rock gardens and containers. The colour range is extensive.

GROWING Plant bulbs 15cm/6in deep in late autumn in groups of 6-12 in well-drained soil in a site sheltered from wind. After flowering, remove the dead leaves and stems. Most species can be left in the ground to flower in subsequent years. Keep free of weeds. Bulbs that must be lifted should be stored in boxes in a dry shed.

PROPAGATION Lift the bulbs carefully when the leaves turn yellow. Remove the offsets, grade by size (discarding the very smallest) and store until planting time at 16-18°C/61-64°F. Replant small offsets 5cm/2in deep.

SPECIES *Tulipa urumiensis (above)*; *T. tarda (above)* forms a rosette of leaves at the base of the stem, with several bright yellow blooms, tipped white, from each cluster; *T. greigii*, height 23cm/9in, vivid scarlet, pointed petals, leaves streaked dark red; *T. pulchella*, violet-red flowers, narrow leaves tinged red; must be lifted.

POSSIBLE PROBLEMS Virus diseases such as cucumber mosaic virus. Mice may eat bulbs in store.

CHOISYA

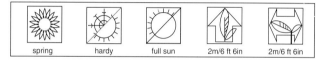

spring	hardy	full sun	2m/6 ft 6in	2m/6 ft 6in

The Mexican orange blossom, *Choisya ternata*, is one of the most accommodating of evergreens. An attractively rounded shrub, its three-part leaves are a dark glossy green and give off a pungent aromatic scent when crushed. A multitude of white, sweet-scented flowers appear in late spring. There are no named varieties.

GROWING Plant in spring in any type of well-drained soil. Full sun is best but semi-shade is tolerated. In cold districts it is best to site plants against a warm, sunny wall. No regular pruning is required, but any frost-damaged leaves or shoots should be cut out in early spring. As soon as flowering is over, cut out any straggly shoots.

PROPAGATION Take 7.5cm/3in cuttings of half-ripe lateral shoots in late summer and place in a peat/sand mixture at 16°C/61°F. When rooted, pot up the cuttings singly and over-winter in a cold frame. Pot on in the spring, set outdoors and plant out the following spring. In cold areas, transfer the pots to a cold frame over winter.

POSSIBLE PROBLEMS Frost damage; honey fungus.

CLEMATIS SPECIES

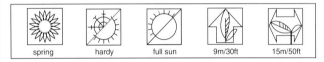

| spring | hardy | full sun | 9m/30ft | 15m/50ft |

Species clematis bear smaller flowers than the showy hybrids, but they are beautiful climbing plants that merit a place in any garden.

GROWING Treat as hybrids. Shade for the root-run can be provided by low shrubs.To prune, remove only weak growths and shorten the remainder by two thirds.

PROPAGATION Species can be raised from seed sown in autumn in pans of compost in a cold frame. After germination, in the following spring, pot up singly and set outdoors, transferring to the permanent site in autumn.

SPECIES *Clematis armandii*, vigorous evergreen, glossy foliage, white saucer-shaped flowers 6cm/2½in across; *C. orientalis*, fern-like leaves, abundant nodding scented yellow flowers in late summer followed by large silver seedheads; *C. tangutica*, grey-green leaves, lantern-shaped yellow flowers in late summer, attractive seed-heads; *C. flammula*, height 3m/10ft, bears a mass of tangled growth at the top with 30cm/12in panicles of fragrant white flowers in late summer/early autumn; *C. montana* (*above*), 12 × 6m/40 × 20ft, easiest species to cultivate, profuse white flowers; the pink-flowered variety 'Rubens' is very popular.

POSSIBLE PROBLEMS Clematis wilt; powdery mildew.

LONICERA

| summer | hardy | semi-shade | 6m/20ft | 3.6m/12ft |

The deciduous climber *Lonicera periclymenum*, better known as woodbine or honeysuckle, is a familiar sight in the wild, twining its stems in strong bands around anything in reach. The cultivated varieties will do the same in the garden, given wires, trellis or an old tree to scramble over. The beautiful tubular flowers have a delicious fragrance.

GROWING Plant from autumn to spring in any type of well-drained soil, previously enriched with humus. Honeysuckles like their roots in shade and the tops in sun. Give a light mulch of leaf-mould or well-rotted compost each spring. Prune after flowering if necessary to remove old wood.

PROPAGATION Take 10cm/4in stem cuttings in summer and place in a peat/sand mixture in a cold frame. When rooted, pot up individually and set outside. Transfer to the flowering site in the late autumn.

VARIETIES 'Serotina' (late Dutch honeysuckle), bushy habit, flowers red outside, cream within; 'Belgica' (early Dutch honeysuckle), red and yellow flowers appear in late spring. These two varieties planted together will provide flowers for a six-month period.

POSSIBLE PROBLEMS Leaf spot; powdery mildew.

POTENTILLA

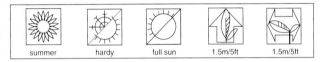

| summer | hardy | full sun | 1.5m/5ft | 1.5m/5ft |

The shrubby cinquefoil, *Potentilla fruticosa*, is a perfect subject for low-maintenance gardens. Totally hardy and requiring virtually no attention if given the correct conditions, it produces five-petalled flowers of yellow, white or orange for the whole summer. There are a number of low-growing varieties which are suitable for ground cover.

GROWING Plant between autumn and spring in light, well-drained soil in full sun. Fewer flowers will be produced in partial shade. To maintain bushy growth, remove old or weak stems at ground level. Cut off the tips of flowering shoots after the blooms have faded. No other pruning is necessary.

PROPAGATION Take 7.5cm/3in half-ripe cuttings with a heel in autumn and place in a peat/sand mixture in a cold frame. Place the rooted cuttings in a nursery bed in spring and transfer to the final positions in the autumn of the following year.

VARIETIES 'Farreri', very delicate foliage, bright yellow flowers; 'Tangerine' *(above)*, low-growing, scarlet in bud, opening to orange, or yellow if in full sun; 'Mandschurica', only 30 × 90cm/1 × 3ft, silver leaves, purple stems, white flowers.

POSSIBLE PROBLEMS Generally trouble-free.

R HODODENDRON

| spring | hardy | semi-shade | 4.5m/15ft | 5m/16ft |

Rhododendrons have much to offer gardeners who must work with acid soil. The magnificent flowers come in an unparalleled range of colours. In size the plants range from as low as 30cm/12in to an imposing 4.5m/15ft or more and spread wide. About 800 species are known and thousands of hybrids have been developed.

GROWING Plant in early autumn in well-drained but moisture-retentive acid soil. Most prefer light shade but hardy hybrids and small-leaved types tolerate full sun. Water well and mulch after planting. Remove dead flowerheads. Prune to restrict growth if necessary by cutting back lightly to a whorl of leaves in spring. Old, straggly hardy hybrids can be induced to make new compact growth if pruned heavily in late winter.

PROPAGATION Increase stock by layering or cuttings. Varieties do not come true from seed.

VARIETIES 'Bluebird', 90cm/3ft high, rich violet flowers; 'Praecox', 1.5m/5ft, rose-purple, very early flowering; 'Scarlet Wonder', 60cm/24in, compact shape. Hardy hybrids (all these up to 4.5m/15 ft, late spring-flowering): 'Cynthia', rose-crimson, vigorous grower; 'Mount Everest', white with red throat, fragrant; 'Purple Splendour', purple marked black.

POSSIBLE PROBLEMS Rhododendron leafhopper causes bud-blast disease; rhododendron bugs suck sap from the leaves.

CLIMBING ROSES

| summer | hardy | full sun | 6m/20ft | 4.5m/15ft |

All gardens, whatever their style, are enhanced by a climbing rose – or two. Climbers with species roses as parents are very vigorous (up to 9m/30ft), bearing 5cm/2in wide cream or yellow flowers in mid summer; climbers bred from hybrid teas are a better choice for more restricted areas such as pillars or fences, and bear flowers up to 12.5cm/5in wide.

GROWING *See Floribunda Roses.* Always plant climbing roses close to their supports. To prune, cut back strong growths after planting to 38cm/15in, weaker ones to within 10cm/4in of the base. Thereafter prune in early spring, leaving the basic framework but cutting back short laterals to 2-3 buds. Tie in new shoots in autumn.

VARIETIES The following are suitable for restricted areas: 'Caroline Testout', profusion of heavily fragrant, double pink flowers; 'Meg', pink and apricot; 'Danse du Feu', double, orange-scarlet; 'Golden Showers', pale gold; 'Parkdirektor Riggers', scarlet; 'Zephirine Drouhin', a bourbon rose, bright pink, fragrant, continuous flowering. Strong growers: 'Mme Gregoire Staechelin', clear pink, fragrant; 'Wedding Day', very vigorous, yellow in bud opening white; 'Mermaid', large, butter-yellow, fragrant, good on a cold wall. 'Fantin Latour' (*above*) double flowers over a short summer period.

POSSIBLE PROBLEMS Climbers are particularly susceptible to powdery mildew.

FLORIBUNDA ROSES

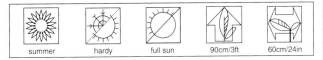

| summer | hardy | full sun | 90cm/3ft | 60cm/24in |

Floribunda roses are derived from the early hybrid teas, and have similar foliage. Whether matt or glossy, there are 7 oval leaflets, sometimes flushed red when young. These roses are very thorny. Flowering twice, in mid summer and early autumn, they bear their 7.5cm/3in wide blooms in large terminal clusters, and are good for borders and decorative hedges.

GROWING If conditions are favourable, roses may be planted at any time from late autumn to spring. Rich, loamy soil gives the best results. Prepare the site by digging it over well and mixing in plenty of well-rotted organic matter. Double-digging is recommended. Make a hole big enough to spread out the roots. Mix a bucketful of peat with a cupful of sterilized bonemeal and place 3 cupfuls of this mixture in each planting hole. Make sure the union of the rootstock and the rose is just below ground level. Give a mulch of partially rotted manure or well-rotted compost every other spring, and a mulch of leaves (rotted or unrotted) each autumn to conserve moisture.

PROPAGATION Increase by budding.

VARIETIES 'Iceberg' (above), 1.5m/5ft, large spray of white, fragrant blooms, good for hedging; 'City of Birmingham', abundant scarlet blooms with wavy petals; 'Korresia', sweetly fragrant, golden yellow.

POSSIBLE PROBLEMS Aphids; caterpillars; sawfly larvae. Black spot; die-back; grey mould; rust; powdery mildew.

69

SPIRAEA

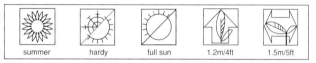

| summer | hardy | full sun | 1.2m/4ft | 1.5m/5ft |

Spiraeas bear tiny star-shaped flowers of white or shades of pink in flat or plume-shaped clusters. They are good subjects for a mixed border and are often grown as decorative hedging.

GROWING Plant between autumn and spring in deep, rich soil in an open sunny position. Prune *Spiraea × bumalda* and *S. japonica* in early spring, cutting back to 10cm/4in from ground level. Remove dead flowerheads. Thin out all species after flowering. Young plants for hedging should be set between 38 and 60cm/15 and 24in apart. Cut back the previous season's growth to within 15cm/6in of ground level after planting. Trim established hedges every year.

PROPAGATION Lift, divide and replant between autumn and spring. Or, take 10cm/4in cuttings of half-ripe side shoots in summer and insert in sandy soil in a cold frame. Transfer to a nursery bed the next spring and plant out in the autumn.

SPECIES *S. × arguta*, commonly known as bridal wreath, a beautiful hybrid bearing umbels of pure white flowers on arching stems in spring, max height 2.4m/8ft, excellent underplanted with crocuses or cyclamen; *S. × bumalda*, hybrid bearing 12.5cm/5in wide heads of bright pink flowers; 'Anthony Waterer' (*above*) is a popular variety with foliage variegated cream and pink when young; *S. × japonica*, maximum height 1.5m/5ft, large pink flowerheads on erect stems.

POSSIBLE PROBLEMS Leaves may be stripped by sawfly.

SYRINGA

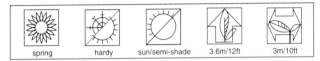

| spring | hardy | sun/semi-shade | 3.6m/12ft | 3m/10ft |

Syringa vulgaris, the common lilac, is one of the best-loved garden shrubs. There are a number of varieties, some double-flowered, all of them fragrant. Lilacs are deciduous, bearing panicles of white, lilac, pink or purple flowers up to 25cm/10in long in late spring.

GROWING Plant in autumn in sun or semi-shade on any type of fertile soil. Lilacs take 1-2 years to become established. Remove all the flowers in the first season to reserve the plant's energies. In later years dead-head after flowering. Remove lower buds and branches to form a single stem if desired. Pull off any suckers that appear. Prune old, straggly bushes in late autumn, cutting back to 90cm/3ft from ground level.

PROPAGATION Take 10cm/4in half-ripe cuttings with a heel in summer and insert in a peat/sand mixture in a propagator at 16°C/61°F. Pot up when rooted and grow on in a cold frame. Transfer to a nursery bed in the spring and grow on for 2 years before planting out.

VARIETIES 'Candeur', cream; 'Firmament', pale blue; 'Massena', deep purple; 'Maud Notcutt', the best white; 'Mrs Edward Harding', double, red; 'Marechal Foch', cerise; 'Primrose', pale yellow; 'Paul Thirion', double, rose-red, very fragrant; 'Souvenir de Louis Spaeth' (*above*).

POSSIBLE PROBLEMS Frost damage leading to grey mould; lilac blight.

71

PESTS & DISEASES

PESTS

PROBLEM	DAMAGE CAUSED	REMEDY
Aphid (greenfly, blackfly)	Sap sucked; honeydew emitted, virus diseases spread	Spray with pirimicarb
Capsid bug	Leaves tattered or with tiny holes	Spray with systemic insecticide
Caterpillar	Leaves, stems, flowers eaten	Spray with permethrin or trichlorphon
Earwig	Flowers, shoot-tips, young leaves eaten	Trap with straw-filled inverted flowerpots on canes among plants; kill with malathion or HCH
Eelworm	Plants weakened, leaves and stems distorted	Destroy infected plants, do not grow again on same site
Lily beetle	Leaves eaten	Spray with pirimphos-methyl
Mealy bug	Sap sucked, virus diseases spread by small insect enclosed in white 'wool'	Spray with malathion
Narcissus fly	No flowers; weak, grassy leaves; maggots in bulbs	Destroy infested (soft) bulbs
Red-spider mite	Sap sucked; foliage desiccated; fine webs spun	Spray with fenitrothion or malathion
Rhododendron bug	Leaves mottled, yellow above and brown below	Spray leaf undersides with pirimphos-methyl
Sawfly	Leaves eaten or rolled under	Spray in late spring with pirimphos-methyl
Scale insects	Sap sucked, virus diseases spread by small limpet-like insects	Spray with malathion
Slugs and snails	Young plant leaves eaten	Scatter methiocarb thinly among plants
Thrips	White speckles, then grey patches on leaves, flowers	Spray with fenitrothion
Vine weevil	Lower leaves holed and notched; grubs on roots, plants wilt	Dust lower leaves and soil with HCH
Whitefly	Sap sucked; virus diseases spread	Spray with permethrin

DISEASES

PROBLEM	DAMAGE CAUSED	REMEDY
Bacterial canker	Leaves full of red holes; stem cankers with oozing gum; general weakening	Cut out infected wood; spray with benomyl
Blackspot	Rose leaves develop black spots; fall early	Rake up and burn all leaves at end of season; spray with bupirimate and triforine
Botrytis (grey mould)	Parts of plant rot, become covered in grey fur	Remove and burn infected parts; spray with benomyl
Bud blast	Rhododendron buds turn brown, develop black pinhead spore capsules and fail to open	Cut off infected buds; spray with fenitrothion to control leafhoppers that spread the disease
Chlorosis	Leaves yellowed; growth stunted on alkaline soils	Grow plants on acid soils. Water with iron sequestrene; feed well
Clematis wilt	Collapse of mature shoots, usually on young plants	Cut back to ground level; water with benomyl
Coral spot	Raised orange pustules on woody stems	Cut out infected wood and burn; paint wood with sealant
Fireblight	Shoots, flowers look burned, turn brown and wilt	Cut out infected stems back to healthy tissue; paint wood with sealant
Fusarium wilt	Lower leaves and stem bases turn brown and rot	Destroy infected plants; do not grow species again on the same ground
Leaf spot	Dark blotches on leaves	Spray with copper fungicide in spring. Prevent by growing on good soil
Lilac blight	Black spots on leaves; shoots wither	Cut out infected wood; spray with bordeaux mixture
Mildew	White powder or downy deposit on leaves and stems	Cut out badly infected growth; spray with benomyl
Peony wilt	Leaf bases of herbaceous peonies turn brown and rot	Destroy infected buds or plants. Prevent by spraying with dichlofluanid
Petal blight	Petals covered by translucent spots, especially in wet weather	Remove and destroy infected blooms
Scab	Reddish-brown spots on leaves; black spots on corms	Dip corms in calomel dust
Virus diseases	Leaves distorted, marbled, yellowed; plant often stunted	Dig up and burn; control insect disease-carriers

GLOSSARY

AERATION Loosening of the soil to admit air.

ALKALINE Used to describe soil with a pH reading above 7.0. A slightly alkaline soil suits most plants.

ANNUAL A plant that completes its life cycle in one growing season.

AXIL The angle between the stem and a leaf, from which further growth arises.

BEDDING PLANT A plant used for temporary garden display.

BIENNIAL A plant that needs two growing seasons to complete its life cycle.

BRACT A modified leaf, which may be coloured and have the appearance of a petal.

COMPOST 1 a mixture of loam, sand, peat and leaf-mould used for growing plants in containers. 2 rotted remains of plants and other organic material.

CROWN The bottom of a perennial such as lupin from which roots and shoots arise.

DEAD-HEADING The practice of removing faded flowerheads in order to prevent seeding, encourage further flowering or to keep a plant looking tidy.

EVERGREEN A plant which bears foliage throughout the year.

FUNGICIDE A substance used to combat fungal diseases.

GERMINATION The first stage in the development of a plant from a seed.

HALF-HARDY Used to describe plants that require protection during the winter.

HARDY Description of plants that survive frost in the open.

HIP Fruit of the rose.

HUMUS The substance remaining when dead vegetable matter has broken down.

INSECTICIDE A substance used for killing insects.

LOAM Soil which is a compound of clay, silt, sand and humus. It is moisture-retentive and mineral-rich.

NODE A joint in a plant's stem from which leaves, buds and side-shoots arise.

PEAT Partially decayed organic matter. Sedge peat is from the roots of sedges growing in bogs.

PERENNIAL A plant that lives for an indefinite period.

PINCHING OUT Removing the growing point of a stem to encourage bushy growth.

PRICKING OUT Planting out seedlings for the first time to larger trays or to a nursery bed.

PROPAGATION Increasing plants.

SPIT A spade's depth - about 25-30cm/10-12in.

STAMEN The male reproductive organ of a flower, arising from the centre of the petals.

TENDER Used to describe any plant susceptible to damage by frost.

TILTH The surface layer of the soil, which is fine and crumbly.

INDEX